REAL VIBE KILLER

POETRY

INSPIRED BY K-POP, DANCE AND PARKOUR

Jae Kha

REAL VIBE KILLER POETRY

Inspired by K-pop, dance and Parkour

© 2021 Jae Kha

Presentation by BookLeaf Publishing
Web: www.bookleafpub.com
E-mail: info@bookleafpub.com

ISBN: 9789358361308
First edition 2021

ACKNOWLEDGEMENT

Hey John — words aren't enough. Thanks for encouraging me to take up this challenge, sticking with me through the entire journey, finessing my graphics and always being up for a boba tea.

Thanks also my friends, all of whom only ever had positive vibes to send my way.

PREFACE

This is the soundtrack of my May 2021.

30 poems inspired by K-pop, dance and Parkour.
I believe in the art of never being still for too long,
which is why I drew on these three elements to help
craft my daily musings.

With a Spotify playlist fuelling my vibes, the moods
of each song, its lyrics and choreography, have been
lightly infused and remixed into poetry form in
these next pages.

Some days, the words on the page pop like bubble
gum and other days they're real vibe killers. Though
in my head, it often feels more like the latter.

May you, who stumbled across this mixtape of
poetry, find that it fills you with colour, rhythm, and
the desire to climb to the top of any wall.

1 / AIRPLANE PT. 2

Auburn and ochre foliage

Rustle and swag

Golden delicious

Sweep me onto a bus
From Seoul into the crimson mountains
Draw the collar of my jacket
Over blush cheekbones
Window shopping in London
Warm my soul with caffeine
Somewhere in Rome

Autumn leaves
Can you be airplane mode
Switch off all my dark clouds

Fly me away to lands of sepia
For I have not left this city
Since the last one and a half laps
Around the sun

2 / BOSS

They say "once is never"
I've never been one to fake it
Don't call myself an ace
Until I ace it

Don't tell me it's not easy
Don't dare plant that thought in my mind

Early days spent spinning on my knees
But now
Don't you notice that I'm looking sky-high
When they speak at me?

Sit your ass back down
The one who leaps first
Wins
I'm the one giving directions

You're the sheep
I'm the wolf

Don't you know
I'm the player
That moves you

3 / SINGULARITY

Six-eight beat

Even-odd-odd

Like too many cups of dirty coffee

My heart pulsates irregular

Hunched in this corner

Oblivious to the mercury slowly dropping

Until I am frozen

A butterfly hug

The only warmth I can trust

Unclenching these fingers
Feeding off this time signature
Gliding with grace
Though our head is full
And mind never still

Such frenetic energy
For a dark, sober mood

Pounding rain distorts the windscreen
An impressionist's dream
There's freedom within these blindfolds
Navigating the lanes
With only my 7th sense

4 / 7TH SENSE

The clock laughs

Can't see its face

But it makes no

mistake

Creeping like a

lizard

Open your eyes

Waiting

For an unmarked delivery van

Though the kettle is already boiling

It's out of my control

Open your eyes

Clapping our hands

Nodding our heads

Body rolls

We're puppets dancing

Open your eyes

I rely on the mirror

Afraid to trust anything else

Configuring the puzzle

Confounded by the shifting pieces

Open your eyes

The figure

Reflects me

Punishing each second of the day

It's life

Not Tetris

Time to awaken from this deep sleep

Look at what's real

5 / CANDY

You can find me
The one always hiding
Something sweet in my mouth

Borderline diabetic
My choice of fuel is toxic
Do you respect my appetite?

Gingerbread house was never my thing
But the candy-littered forest trail seemed dope
The Pied Piper to this mouse

I accept payment these days
In boba and chocolate
Inject it the way you sniff wine

Thumb over camera lens
Jiving here like groovy
Popping that choc rock

If you catch my eyes
Shimmying by
They'll be candy-high crazy

6 / MAFIA IN THE MORNING

Mafia, wake up!
Sì, but we're changing the rules
Killing is no longer fun
Ruins the bank accounts, fools

Roll up, roll up!
The medic doesn't know he's a pimp
Heads down, thumbs up
An uninformed majority of wimps

Rise up, rise up!
Fear of something, just ain't living
The protest is silenced
Deaf on the ears of the sleeping

Yawn!
Sun shines, but head is in a knot
Stretch my arms out
A jab marks the spot

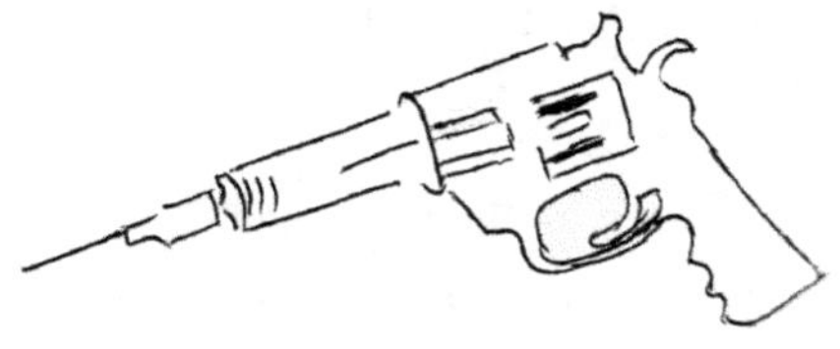

An informed minority

Lurking Mafiosi

A matter of time

Until you get marked as their property

In the daylight I point at their temples

Cock my fingers

When night falls, I fall

The Matrix turns to winter

Where's Wally?

A poker face amongst the sheep

Friends, wake up

Mafia, go to sleep

7 / MAKE A WISH

Make a wish, make a wish
Who are you?
Doesn't matter, make a wish

Monday, come now, make a wish
I dream of sharp fluidity and hands that glide
Then don't think the movement, be the movement

Tuesday, hit that line, make a wish
Give me control, mastery of isolations
Remember, you are your only competition

Wednesday, I'll take you anywhere so make a wish
I need body rolls, an infusion of sass
With precision, comes confidence

Thursday, put your hands together, make a wish
Two words, cat pass
Train so that you can never get it wrong

Friday, back it up, dial it up, make a wish
Cure this exhaustion, I'm feeling so sapped

Être et durer

Saturday, we got this, make a wish
If only I could freestyle, make shapes and just groove
Do one thing every day that scares you

Sunday, 100%, make a wish
Happiness and the simple things that spark joy
If you don't like where you are, move

Make a wish, make a wish
Are you real?
Put it out to the universe, make a wish

8 / GOOD BOY

I'm the cool kid, yo
Everyone would follow
What's changed now, my flow?

Click, I'm off the leash
I could escape and be free
But something binds me

Day dreams just go on
Past life, did I do a wrong?
One more, K-pop song

Bow wow, oh master
Former gangster and player
I'm a lil' hamster

Big up, puff my chest
But when she leaves on a quest
I'm just such a mess

What reason think of
Her scritches and hugs are rough
Yikes… think I'm in love!

New found kind of joy
Not used to being a toy
I'm a good, good boy

9 / WELCOME TO MY PLAYGROUND

You're invited

Passcode is "Play"

Won't encounter no bouncers

Just an obstacle

To the set the scene

And get your buy-in

Only condition of entry

No negativity

Nor real vibe killing energy

Karaoke

Trees to climb

Ninja walls

Bouldering mats

Pop art

Idols and rockstars

All the world's a stage

How about we dance?

Bartender

Make that snob dance too

Channeling Burning Man

In our neo city

We have more than 24 hours

This ain't no child's play

The seeds are finally blooming

In the garden of the sentient

We can have it all

Limitless

Why do you think

You have to choose your cake?

10 / UN VILLAGE

Soaked leaves chase each other

Down the footpath

I realise

Everywhere feels like

Paris in the rain

Two hours through a tunnel

Step out into the city before sunrise

Charming apartment

Winding staircase

Jogging through empty streets

To see each other

Shared umbrella

Trench coats

We could be a watercolour

Crêpes on the street

Whatever the mood

By the Notre Dame

Long before she blazed

Like da Vinci decoded
Puddles underneath our feet
We danced with no choreography
Feeling in Louvre

Green grass shooting up fast
In the autumn drizzle
Covering all our tracks
But we know
Everywhere feels like
Paris in the rain

I might not have deserved it
Our precious time
It was simple
A treat

Maybe next time Hannam-dong
Another UN Village
High up on some hill
Watching the street lamps
Touch the rain with their light

Cos everywhere feels like…

11 / MONSTER + INFINITY

Waiting for the rumble
Shadows waking up
Ruler of all monsters

Every day surrounded by the wicked
Just because you don't hold a knife
Doesn't mean you're not a killer

I won't bother trying to warn ya
I'm clocking you
Counting your sins

Thanos was misunderstood
Batman saw it, one foot in the dark side
Blocking the sun out with his wings

Kylo and his grandpa
Killed off not by false ambitions
But the writer's pen

Abused of their ideology
Toyed with by monsters

Everyone surrounds me

Smiling sc innocently

Suppressed only by law and order

They're coming

Dripping on you

Join the walking dead at the border

It's too late

Face the mirror

See the one who set the trap

Don't run

Look me in the eye

There's no turning back

12 / PUNCH

Get up

Nurse the bruises and the wounds

They will heal

Don't try to seek help

Everyone looked away from your abuse

No more excuses to stay

Get out of this place

There are two paths

Don't take the one signposted "Victim"

It's time to reinvent yourself

Return on your terms

Get in the ring

Licking your lips

Uppercut jab cross hook

Floater butterfly

Stinger bee

Throw it

13 / NO MANNERS

A glitch
That I don't want to debug

Indie rock chick
Loyal to the core
Interrupted

Rude
Assaulting me with content
Gyrating on the stage

This duality is dangerous
Aegyo one minute
Fierce the next

Sweet and salty
Addictive combination
Aesthetic of my failure

I became a fan

They said, "Welcome

There's no exit"

Dearest emo hour

Chilling on the southeast corner of the clock face

Can you provide me some company tonight?

My heavy lids make like long exposure

Pulling the oncoming high beams

Into elegant white lines

A kettle boils in the distance

Shift workers curse

Your savage aura

Will you cast me some moonlight

To navigate these roof tiles

Where I can lay back and touch the black sky

The days sap my chi

So I sink into my pillow

Every time you come out to play

Reclaiming the empty streets

Carving and curves over cold tram tracks

Sliding down skatepark bowls

I'll bring the stories
You set the ambience
Let's unwind together again someday

15 / DOMINO

Runs with the boys

Plays with their toys

Shortcomings puncture her ego

Kills her soul to conform

Conspiracy as a platform

Yet everyone's judgment renders her hollow

Craves like an extrovert

Collapses as an introvert

Blanket of loneliness and shadow

Independent and confident

It's so tiring being out front

Just want someone worthy to follow

Gasping for air

With strength comes despair

In so many ways this was all just for show

Integrity is but a deck of cards

This mask is forged with glass

"By Wednesday you're laughing again," said Monroe

Throw a lifeline before it's too late

A love that can help shoulder this weight

Change key to major on the piano

A warm breeze

An honest hand to squeeze

A soft landing to fall on. Domino

16 / KICK IT

Sprint at the wall
Like it's platform 9 and 3 quarters

Knuckles turn white
Gripping the edge

Foot slides
Knee bruises
Body slam

Was always more Bruce Lee
Than Jackie Chan

Rev up those guts
Chase that barricade
Fast as you can get

Bass kick swing it up higher
Shimmy shimmy shimmy up
If you can no longer pop it

Top of the wall

Trippiest view of all

17 / HOT SAUCE

Is this bottle ketchup
Or something rather nasty
Don't spoil my broth
Ever heard of hangry?

Some like it spicy
But there's no Tabasco in me
I'm all about the flavour
Wait, what level is this kimchi?

You keep stirring, stirring
There are consequences if you burn me
My temperature is rising
Seems you wanna be my enemy

Feel the frost in the air
I'll control the mercury
Drop your Scoville from 750,000
Down to negative territory

This dish is already intense
Five senses fragrant synergy
Toast to the gods
Now bon appétit

37

Tiger eyes in the morning, awake before the alarm sings. Telepathy. Can't anticipate how the day will unfold, brisk beanie walk to clear the clouds. Force field. Sell soul to the company, eyes loopy from the screen. Laser vision. Cramming last minute action, into a schedule booked out weeks in advance. Time travel. Drug deals at the 11th hour, after the pharmacist has gone home. Telekinesis. Drag self behind the wheel, moving dangerously. Invulnerability. Balance on rails, scale some concrete. Super strength. Play with pup, write poetry. Healing. Never bored, never mundane. Flight. It's not the end of the day, until I say so. Cosmic.

19 / SWITCH

Haters, read down

Don't listen to K-pop

You are living in a cave if you

Immerse yourself in hours of mirrored dance

practice videos

Imagine the horror, of a world where you can't

Accept that you suck at dance

Don't let yourself

Spend money on idol-sponsored face masks

Your complexion won't improve if you don't

Stop eating jjajangmyeon

Life's too short to

Dive into pop-colour K-culture

Run from a challenge

Do not attempt to

Turn on a light switch

Who knows what you might encounter if you

Get curious

It makes sense that you should

Keep avoiding the obstacles

You'll reach a dead end if you

Take the path less travelled

Don't look up

You'll regret it if you

Switch

Dreamers, read up

20 / DON'T CALL ME

Are we in this together?

Through mud and stormy weather

It's okay if that's not the case

You just have to lay it straight

Lock stock, break these chains forever

Came here with no clothes

No VVS diamonds or 24-carat gold

A house doesn't make a home

You stubbornly keep calling my phone

Your true voice just echoes so cold

Give work to the busiest one

You'll sell me the sun

A smile so sweet

When eyeing fresh meat

Sick of all your trash, gotta run

Escape to the mountains to be free

Find company amongst the birds and trees

Limited network coverage

Time wasters can't leave a message

Until they drop the "I" and exist as "we"

21 / 2 KIDS

Everything is just perspective
Restrictions on our freedoms as a collective
Gives rise to clean air, each inhale fresh and electric
Streets to jaywalk, such an incentive
Schedules erased of FOMO irrespective

We can walk lightly resurrected
Clouds over our heads redirected

2 kids play with joy so infective
We are young and dumb and festive
Dive to the grass and roll like it's reflexive
Launch onto steel nets at a pace that's explosive

Change pace, balance and be attentive

2 kids seize a moment to be nondirective
Traversing the perimeter of this field is salaciously
addictive
Limits exist only in your mind, a mirage conjured by
the deceptive
In this playground, there's no limits on the creative
Though, slipping on dog shit is a genuine
prospective

Move, no matter your style, be routine or be
inventive
Move, trial and error to determine what's effective
Generate memories for a retrospective

2 kids
Conquering fear is our objective

45

Patience
Not in my genes
Counting down til Thursday
The next episode gets released
Webtoon!

Hero
You will suffer
Just how the plot arc flows
I'm on your side til the last scene
Battle!

UGH
#@%!
!! ゴゴゴ
#&#@

23 / SUPER CAR

Move vroom
A sound so satisfying
Let's roll, zoom zoom
Speakers surround, amplifying

Chase the green lights
All lanes, post-to-post illumination
Free to the boldest at night
No split-second hesitation

Like a decent pair of shoes
Taking me on amazing journeys
Super car, wherever we choose
We'll join the birds that are early

Accelerator knows my mind
Supercharged athlete
Windows down, unwind
Dancing in the backseat

24 / TIGER INSIDE

Ode to my obsession

The rhythm of how a cat passes

Sailing over that barricade

With feline grace

Need to wake up this tiger
Untie these shackles
Put the roar
Back into these shoulders

Forgive me if I snarl at you
It's the kitty caged inside me
Trying to confront the nemesis head first
To commit to the drop

Bruised ego
Pulling back instead of yanking through
Shins colliding with concrete
Scars to prove the shame

I keep prowling the perimeter
The law of the jungle
Does not escape me
Cat the pass and be set free

25 / CHERRY BOMB

Criminal thoughts, chase havoc

Hellish clap, hot fireworks

Explosions, everywhere Kapow!

Rebel without a cause, raise the roof

Rooting for Guy Fawkes, rules don't apply

You only live once, yeah my mind is delinquent

Blow down the house

Obliterate the safe zone

Molotov cocktails

Bombs away!

Paying for the right
To enter the escape room
Seeking to escape
What is this madness?

Minimalist
Forever needing to be
ready
To leave it all behind

Wanting to let go
Of something
That I never had
To begin with

Make a scene at the exit
Don't want to escape quietly
Because who doesn't want
To be remembered?

Entrance to the magic shop

Open to all dreamers

If you seek directions

Ask your inner child

Butter beer

A thrilling castle rollercoaster

Cajun sauce dipped McNuggets

Anime worlds

Care parcel full of Swiss chocolate
Stories hidden within
Pages of a book
Dancing light of the afternoon sun
A perfect voice

Step outside the front door
See the moon glide
Into the earth's shadow

Religion
Science
Perhaps magic

Should I turn the words upside down
Write "I'm fine"

It's artificially warm
Though the atmosphere
Is chilly to touch
When I press the "off" button
The bitterness of winter
Rushes in

I can't stand the cold
It cuts to the bone
Doesn't matter which way I turn
The stiff air
Is like darkness creeping

A matchstick
Like a hand reaching out
Can it break through this?

Fight the numbness

Choreography

Spins and sweat energy

Spin "Save me" upside down

Snug affectionate poetry

29 / END OF A DAY

Nearing the end of this journey
Will the destination be
As memorable as the road we took?

Push the chair away from the desk
Muscles tight and stiff
Stretch it out
Press our sore backs to the floor

You did a good job
The prize will be waiting

An impressive point has been made
Day after day
Through poetic runes

I no longer want to
Close the door to the day
Later than other people

Tomorrow we sign off on this chapter
Musings before midnight settled

There's time to refuel

Before the phoenix rises

Mic drop

30 / BACK DOOR

Let's go, 3, 2, 1

Access all areas

I'm the most authorised person in the room

What did I just flash?

Like a boss

More than one VIP pass

Move aside or follow me

Welcome to my playground

Vroom

Crash through the gates like I'm a super car

On the other side of the fence now

Make no mistake and don't hesitate

Don't call me unless you wanna come in

Hop on this airplane pt 2

Good boy

Throw cherry bombs over our shoulders

Blow down the first domino

Monster + infinity

A candy trail of destruction

It's been a while

I need to adjust my eyes

Switch on the bass and the beat

This freedom's causing delirium

My 7th sense is pounding

Tiger inside my head is roaring

My lungs hurt

Overdosing on the sudden adrenaline

Hot sauce overflowing

I used to save the best

Tell myself paradise could wait

Time waits for no one

This magic shop was always here

Make a wish

Convert my save me into I'm fine

Singularity of purpose

To run, to dance, to scream at the top of our lungs

This party doesn't need no manners

Killjoys beware

Cos at the end of a day

We're all mafias in the morning

I'm determined

A levanter

I'm a boss

People call me superhuman

So I'll build us a UN Village

A place open to 2 kids or a billion

1:27PM, 4AM or anywhere on the clockface

Where we can just kick it

Regenerate like an action figure

So, you wanna come in?

www.ingramcontent.com/pod-product-compliance
Lightning Source LLC
LaVergne TN
LVHW021236200726
843509LV00012B/1502